Blossom
FLORIST

GRAYSCALE COLORING BOOKS

VOLUME 1.

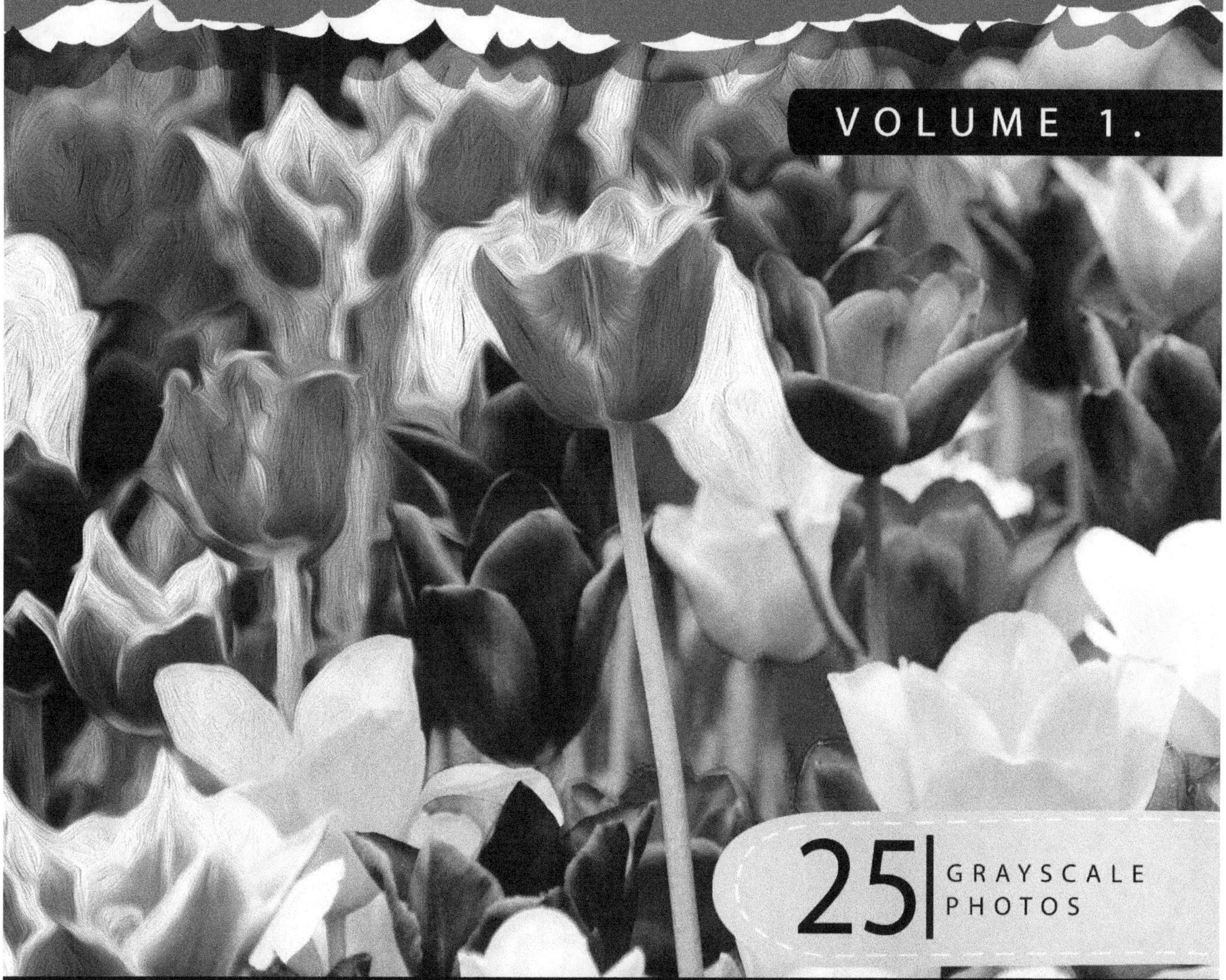

25 | GRAYSCALE PHOTOS

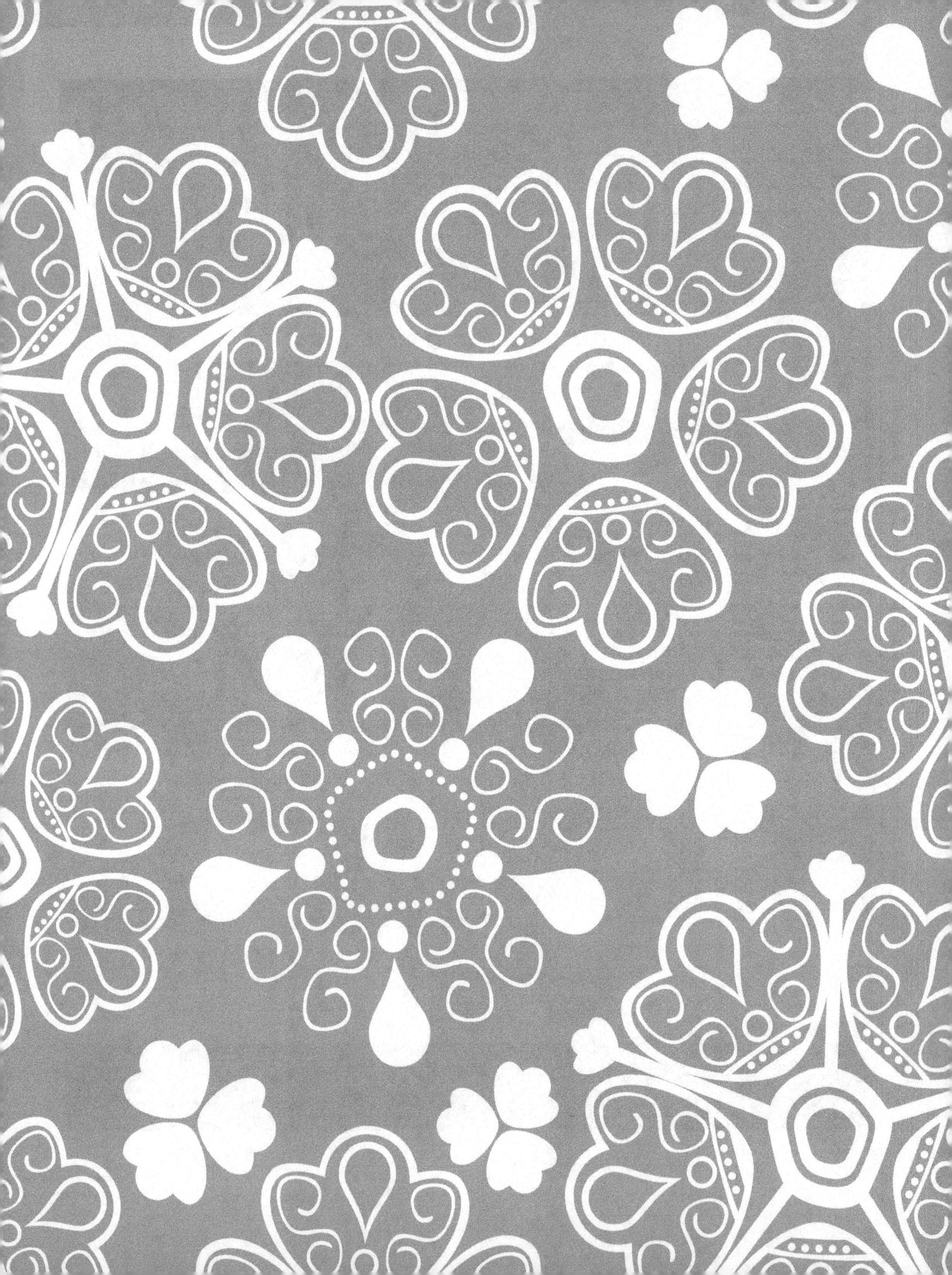

COLOR TEST PAGE

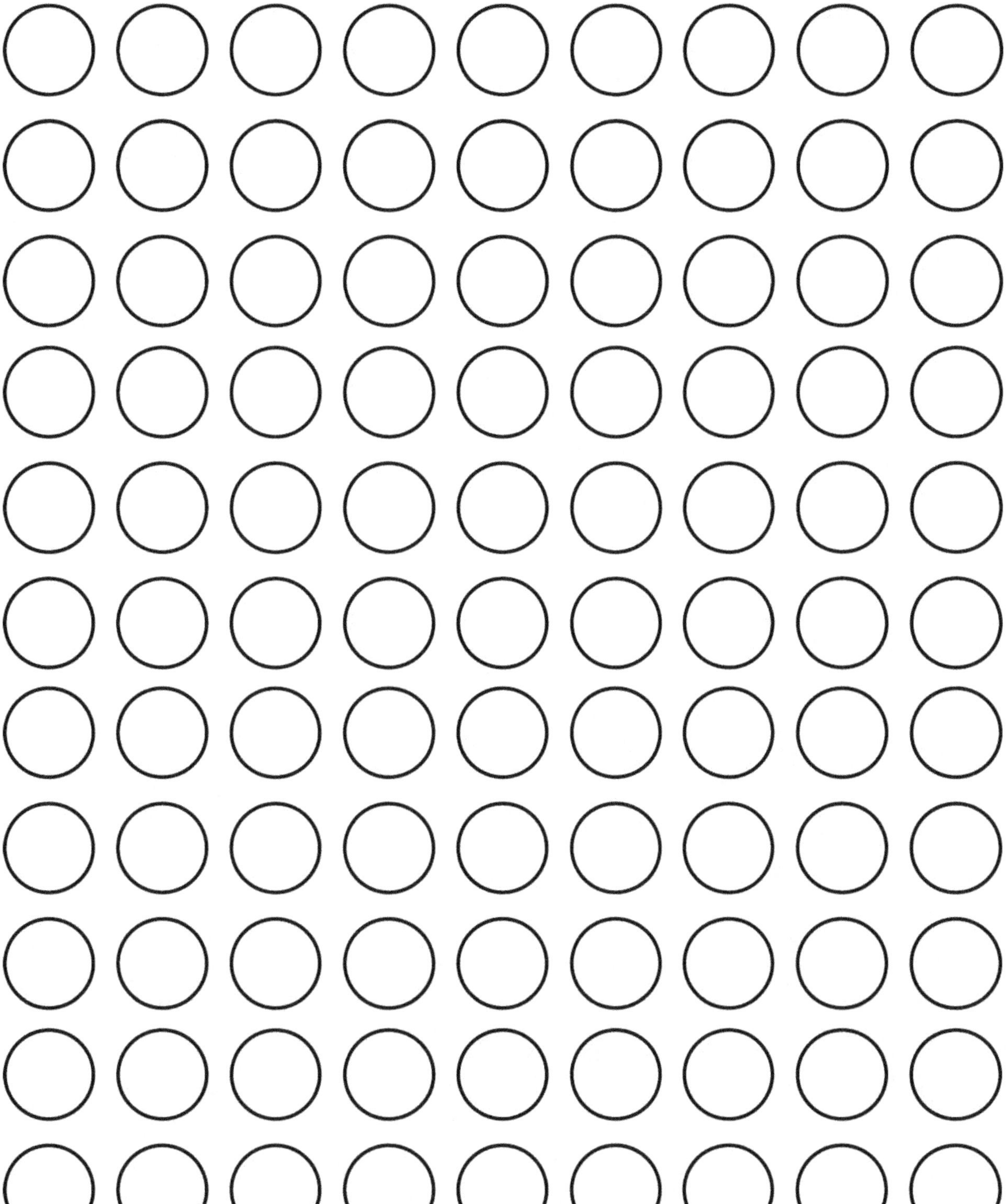

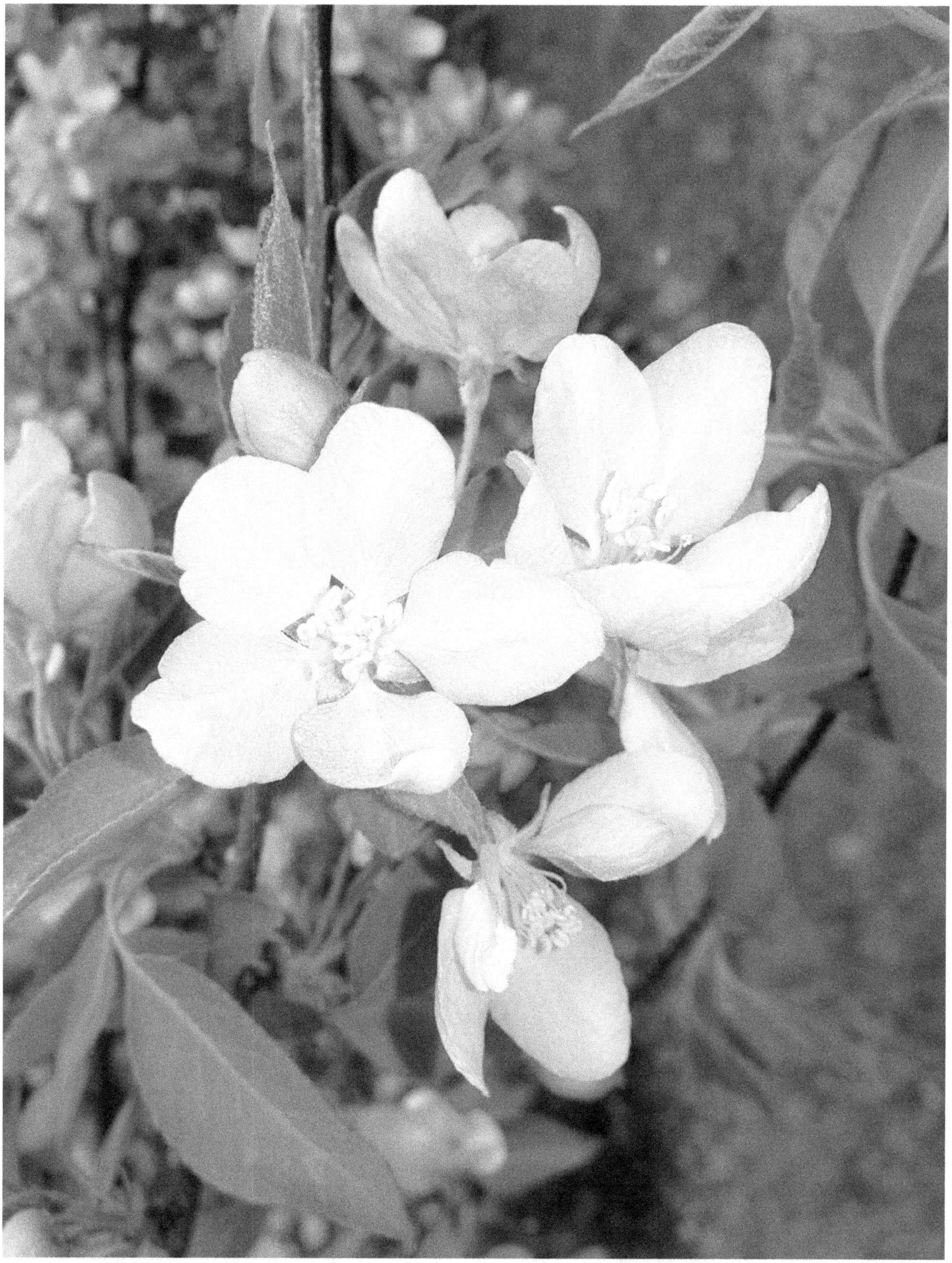

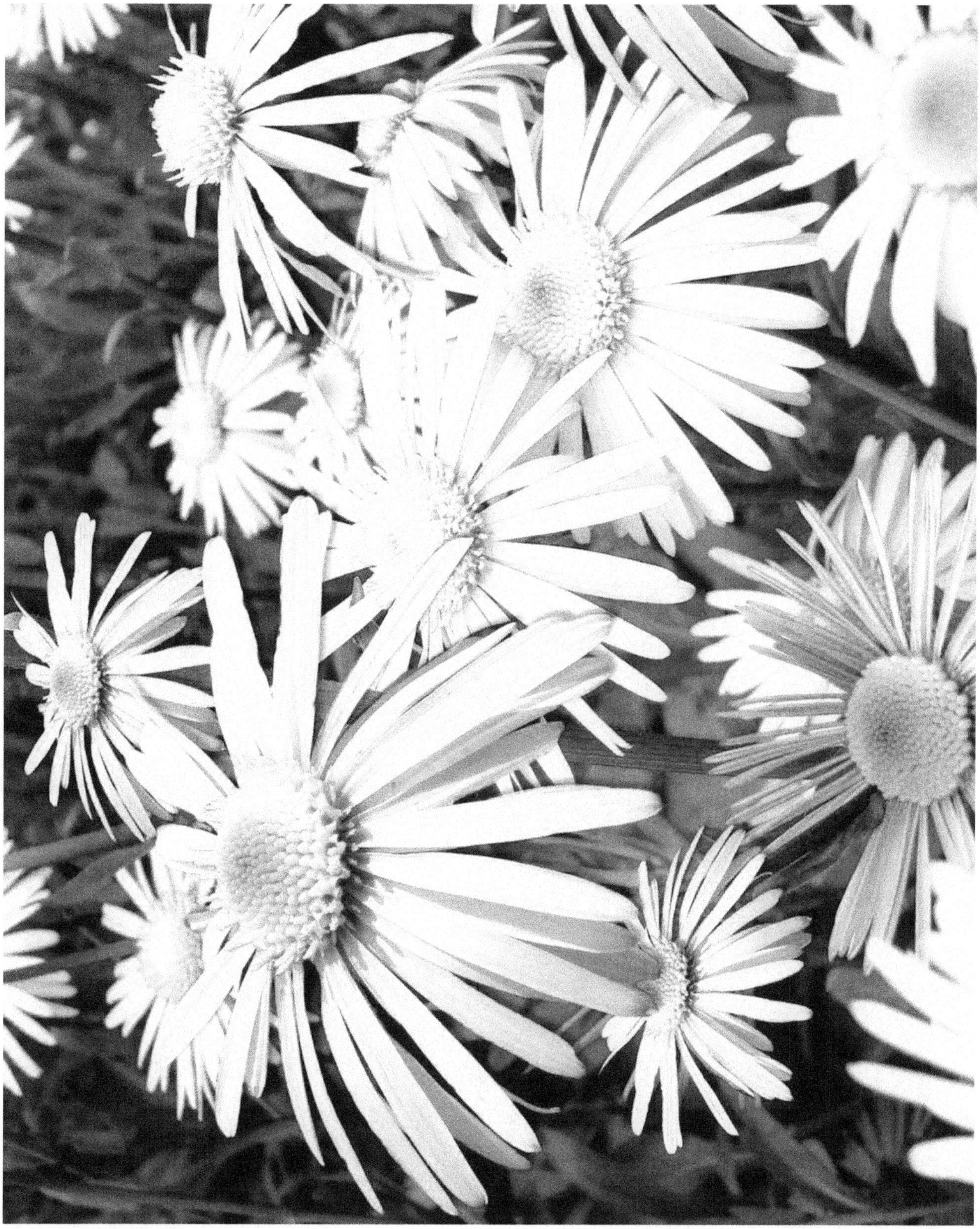

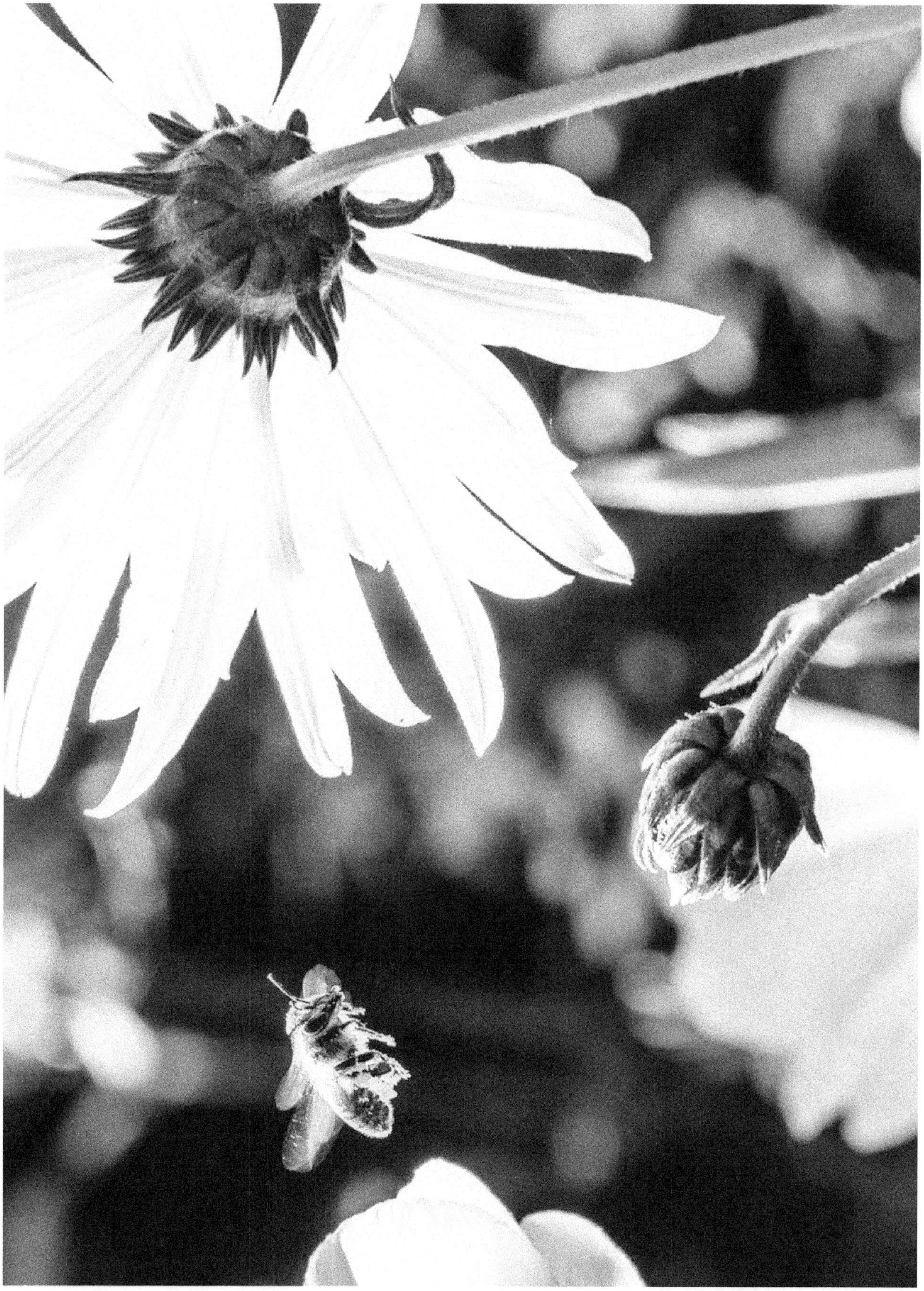

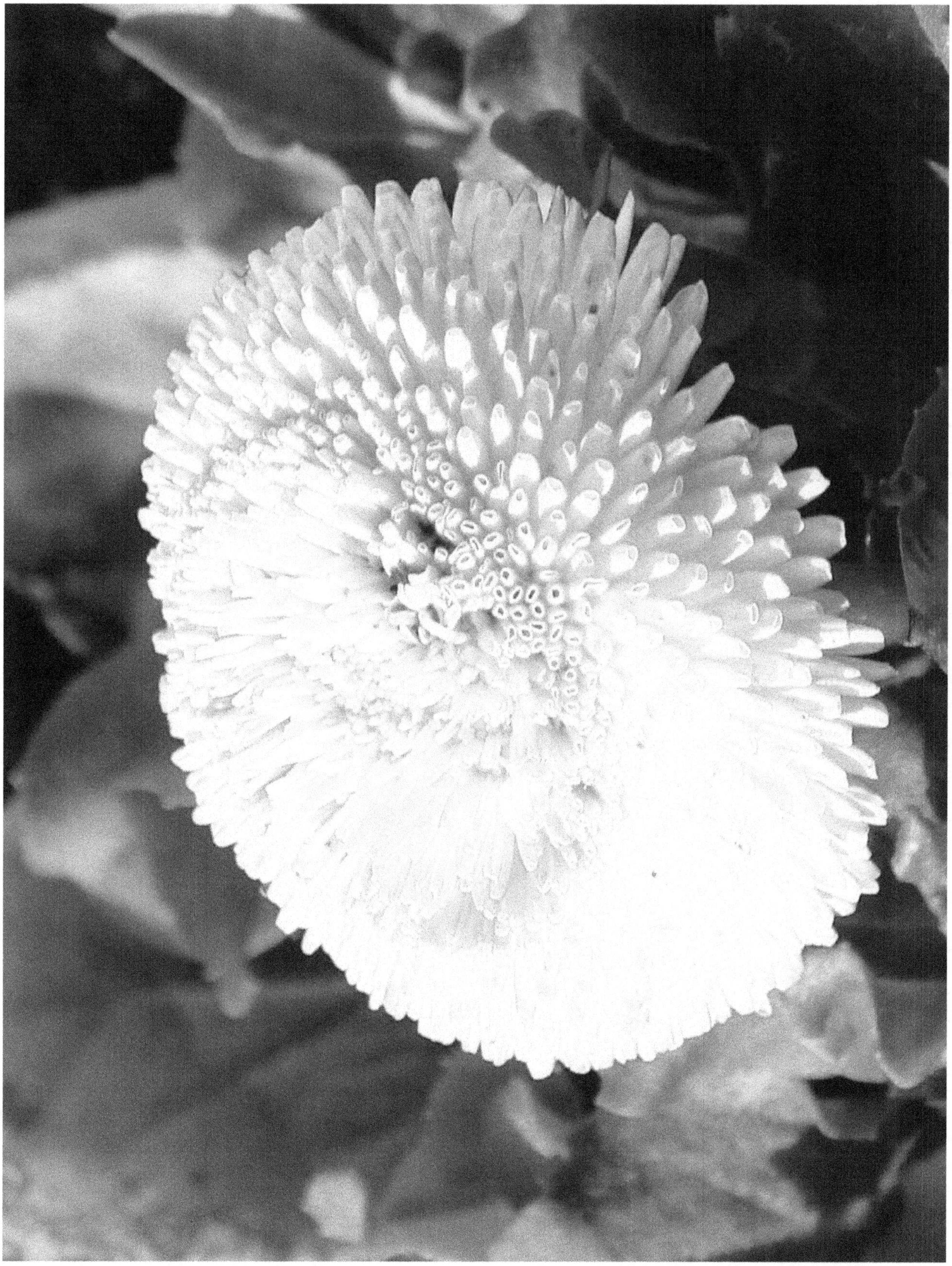

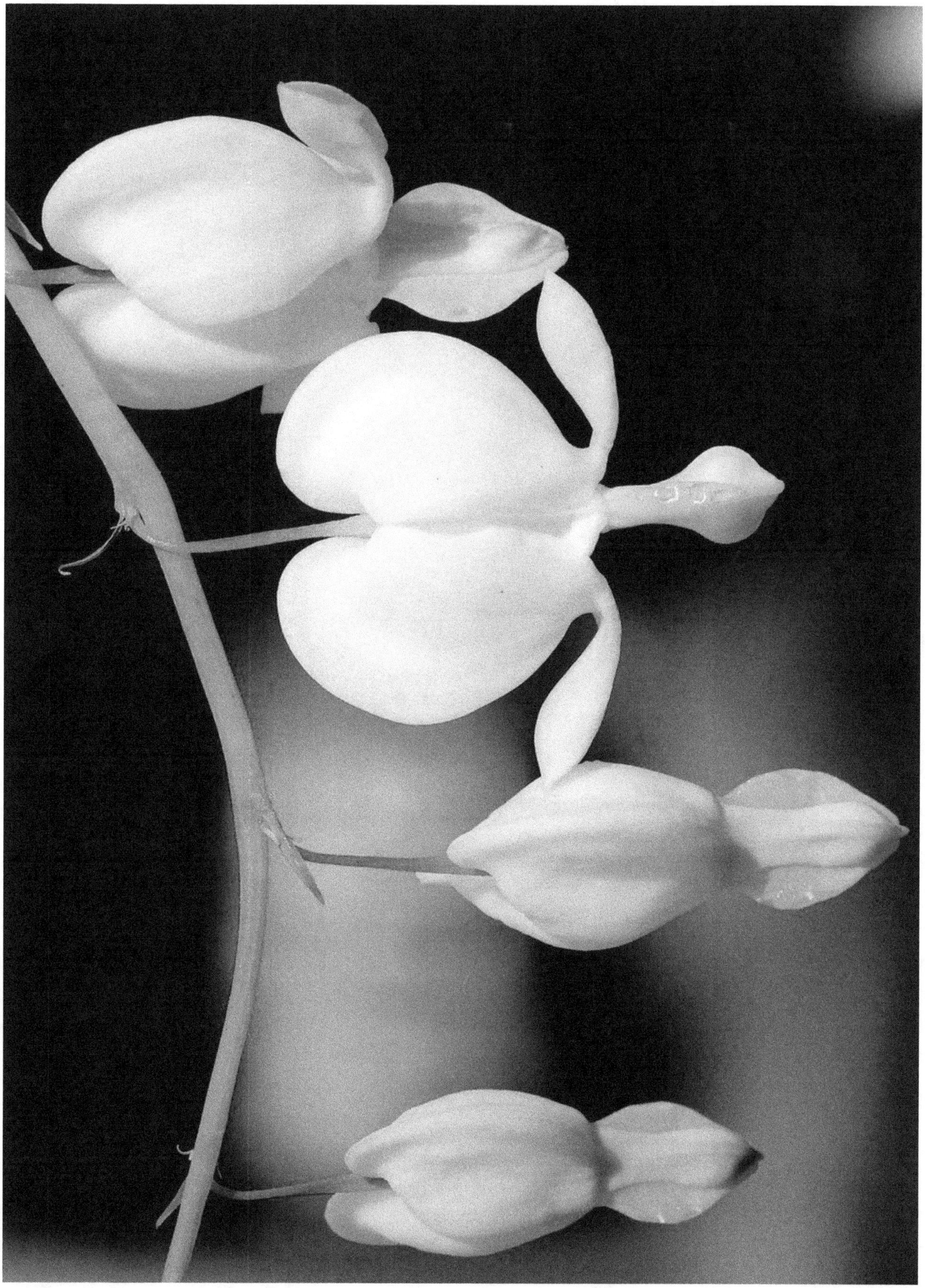

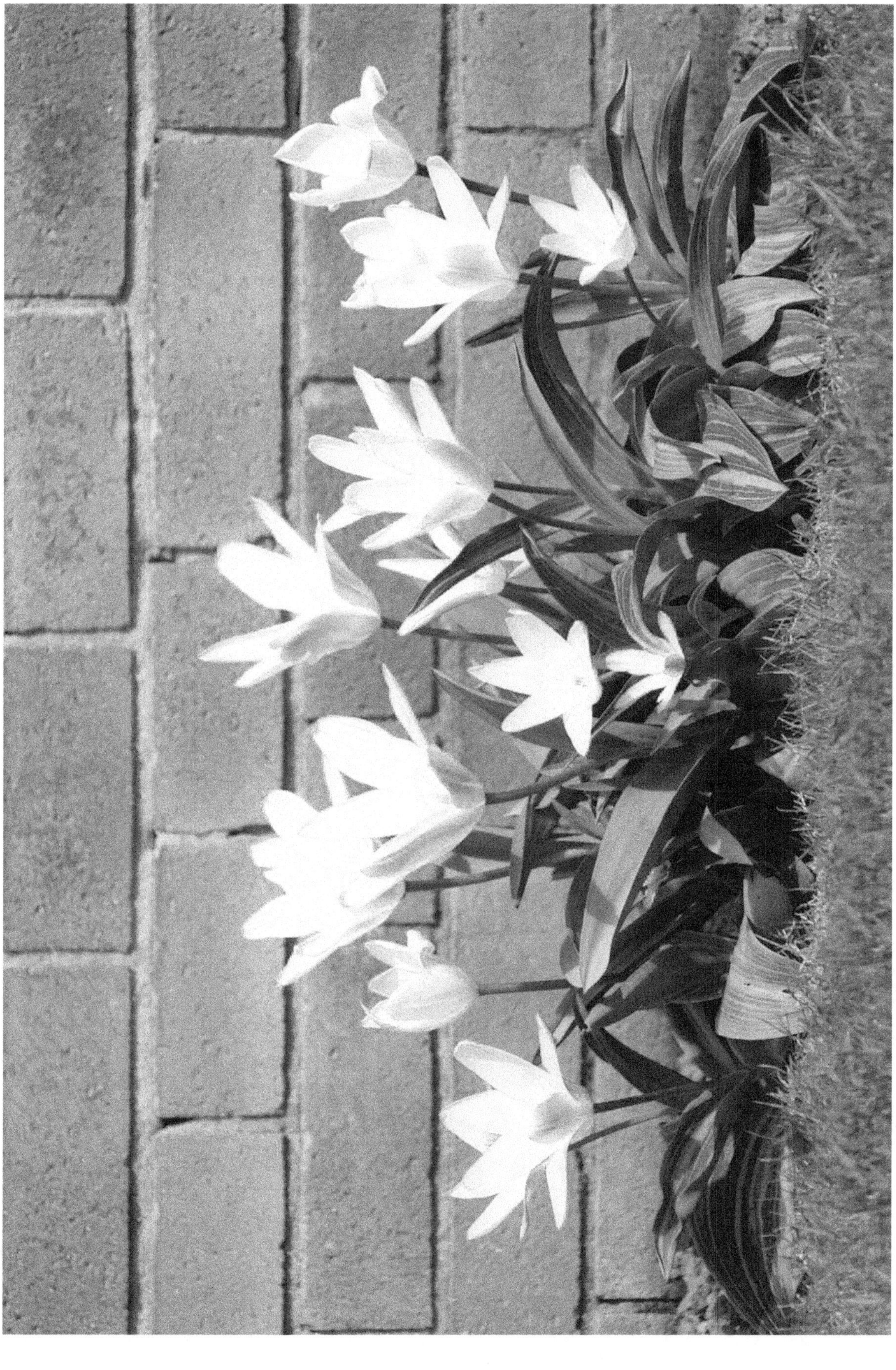

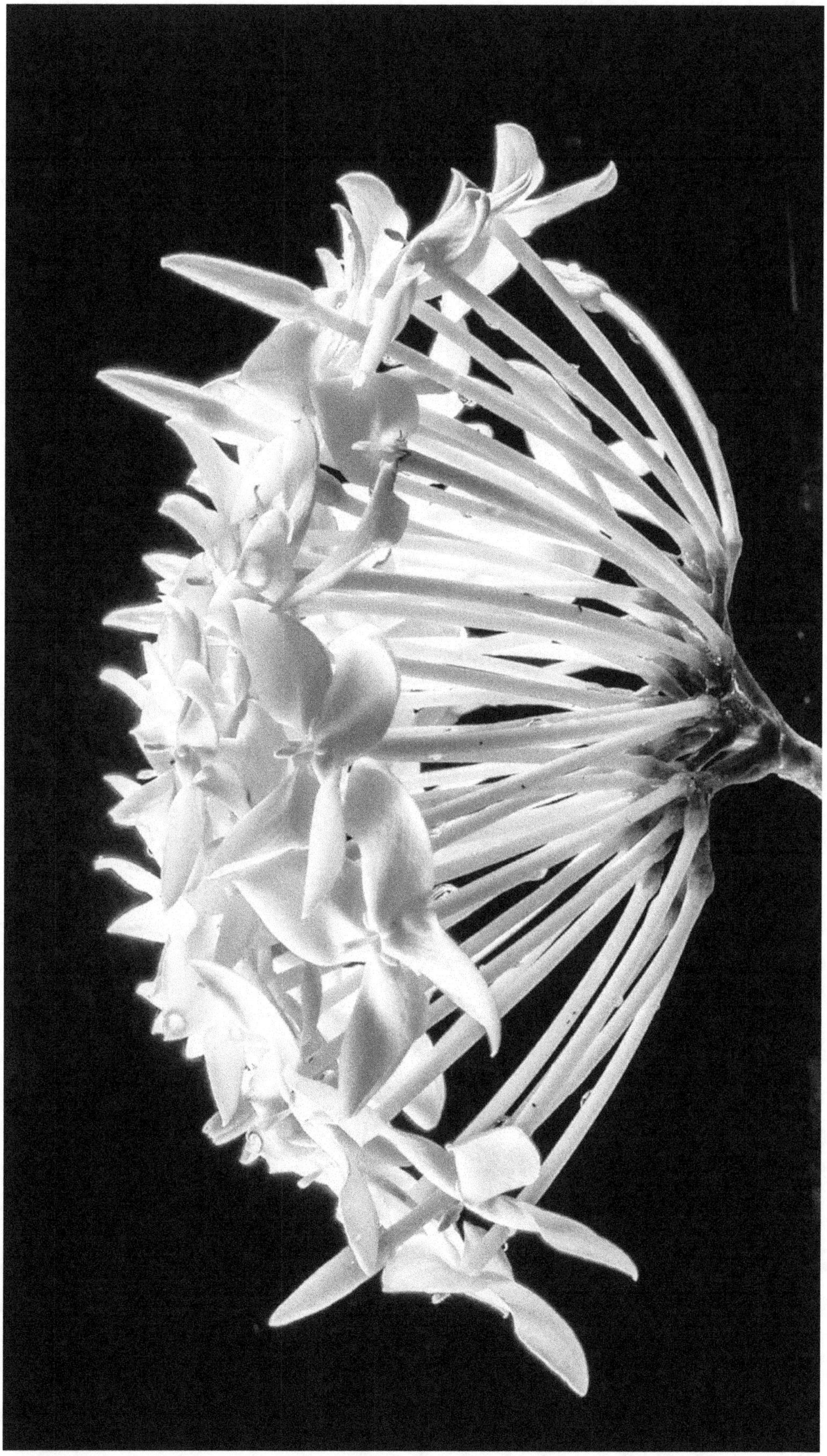

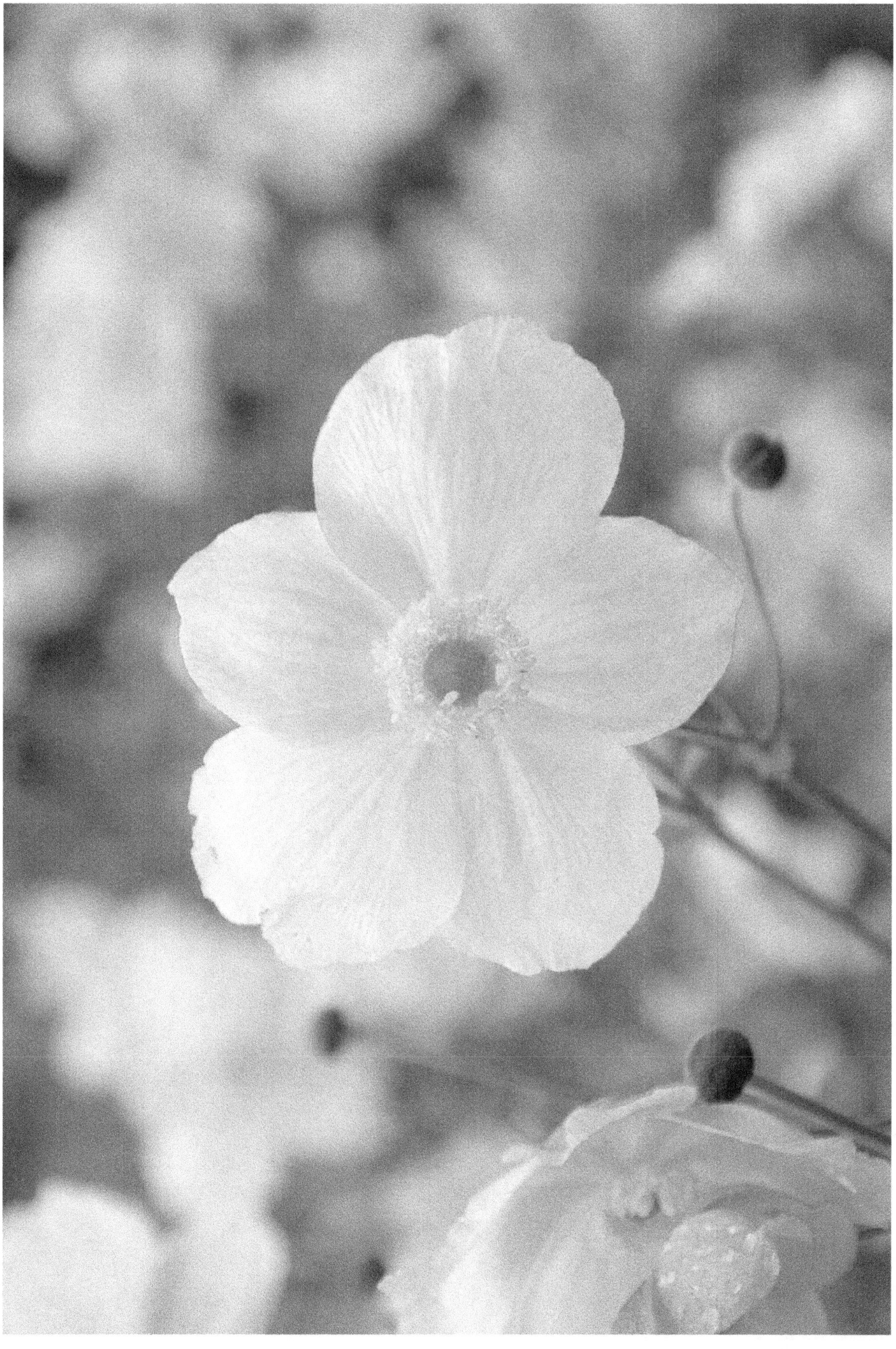

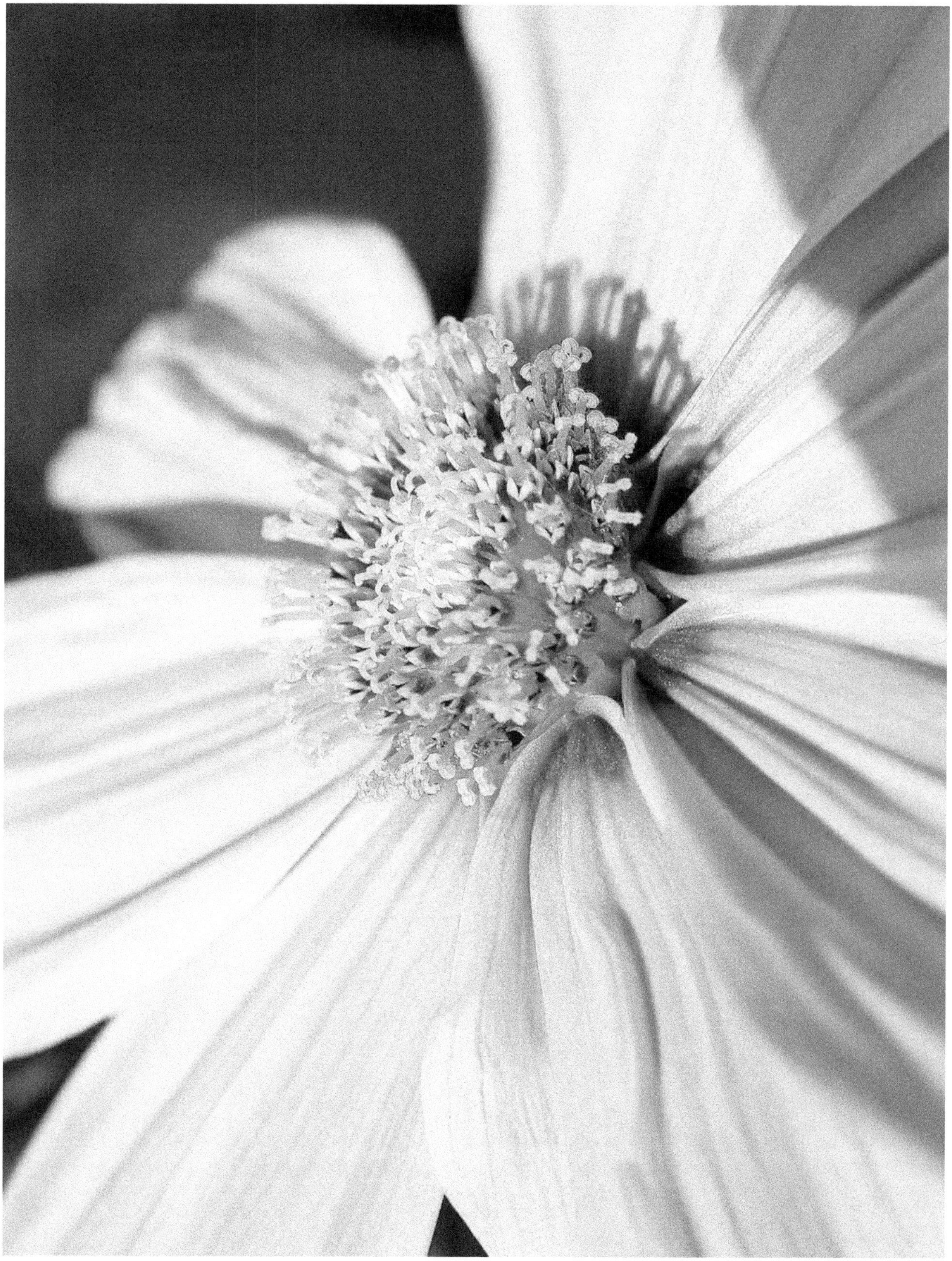

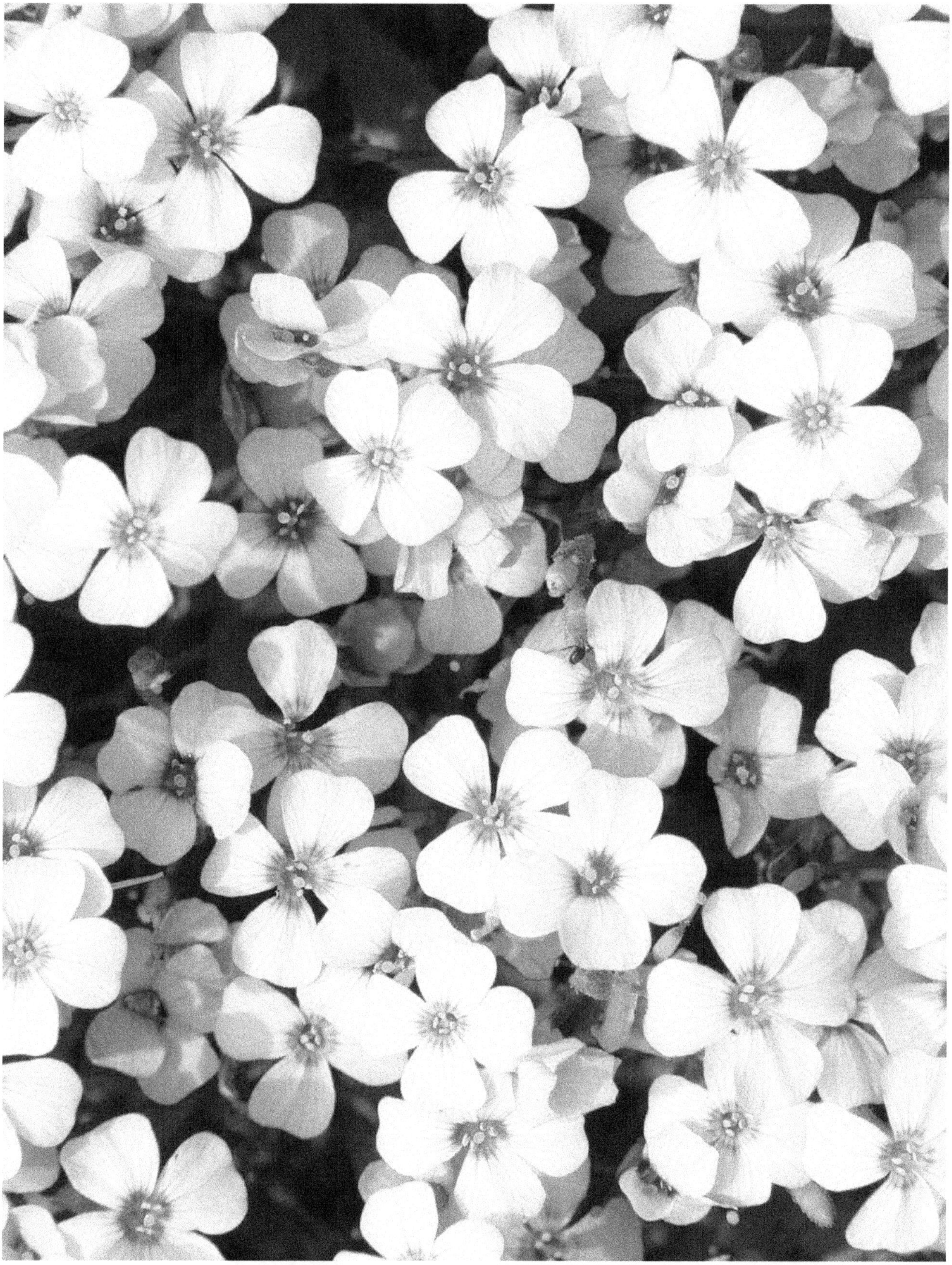

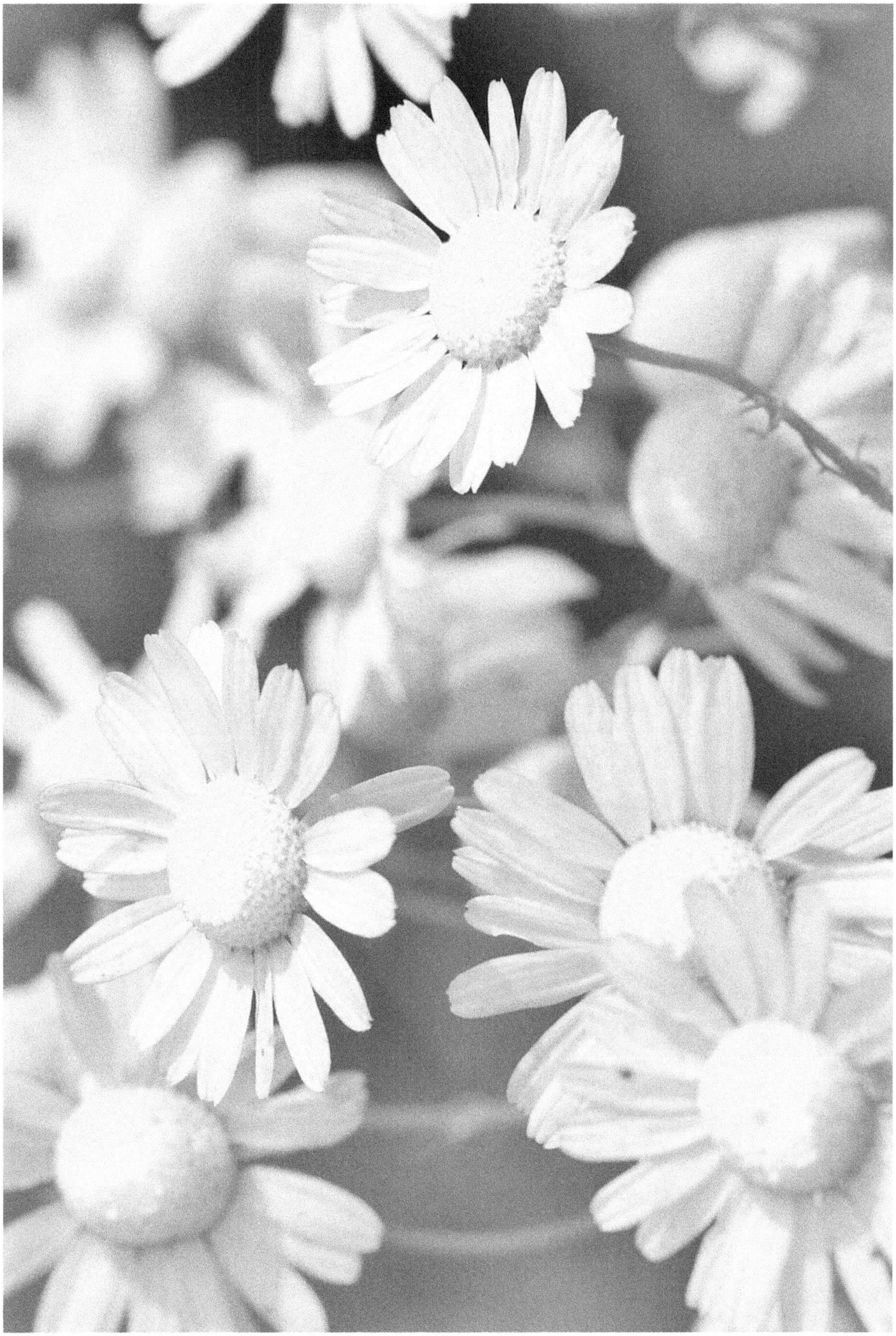

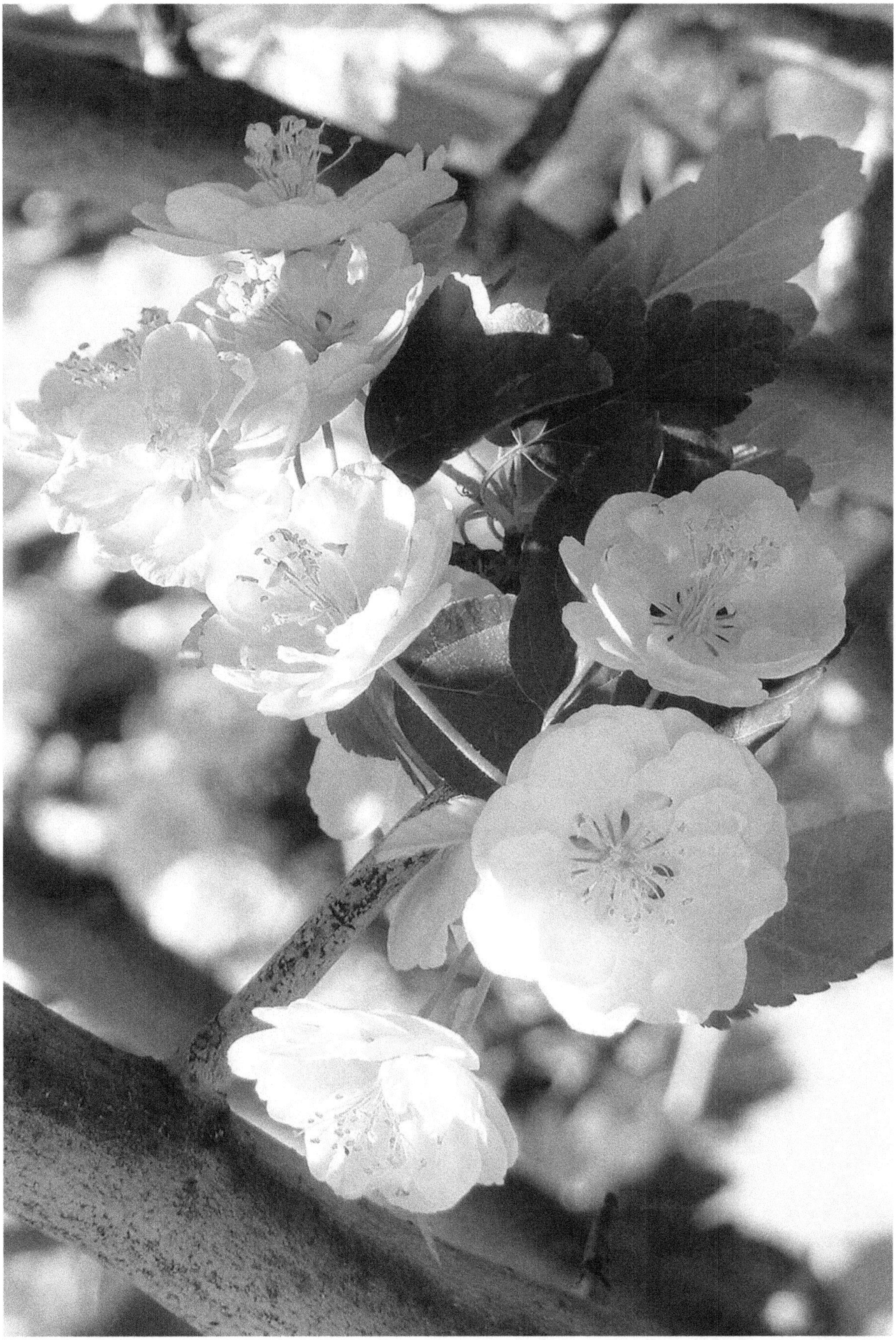

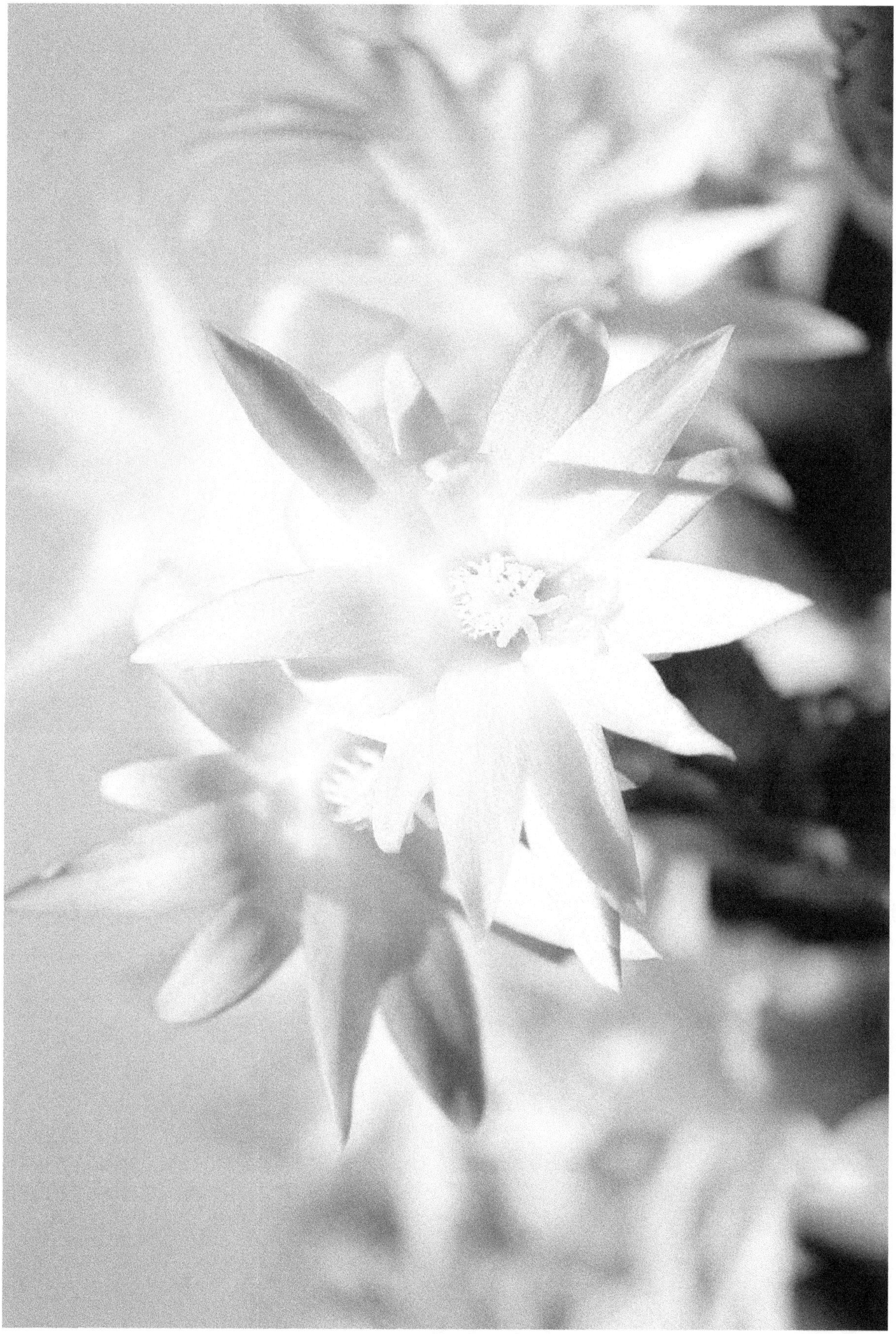

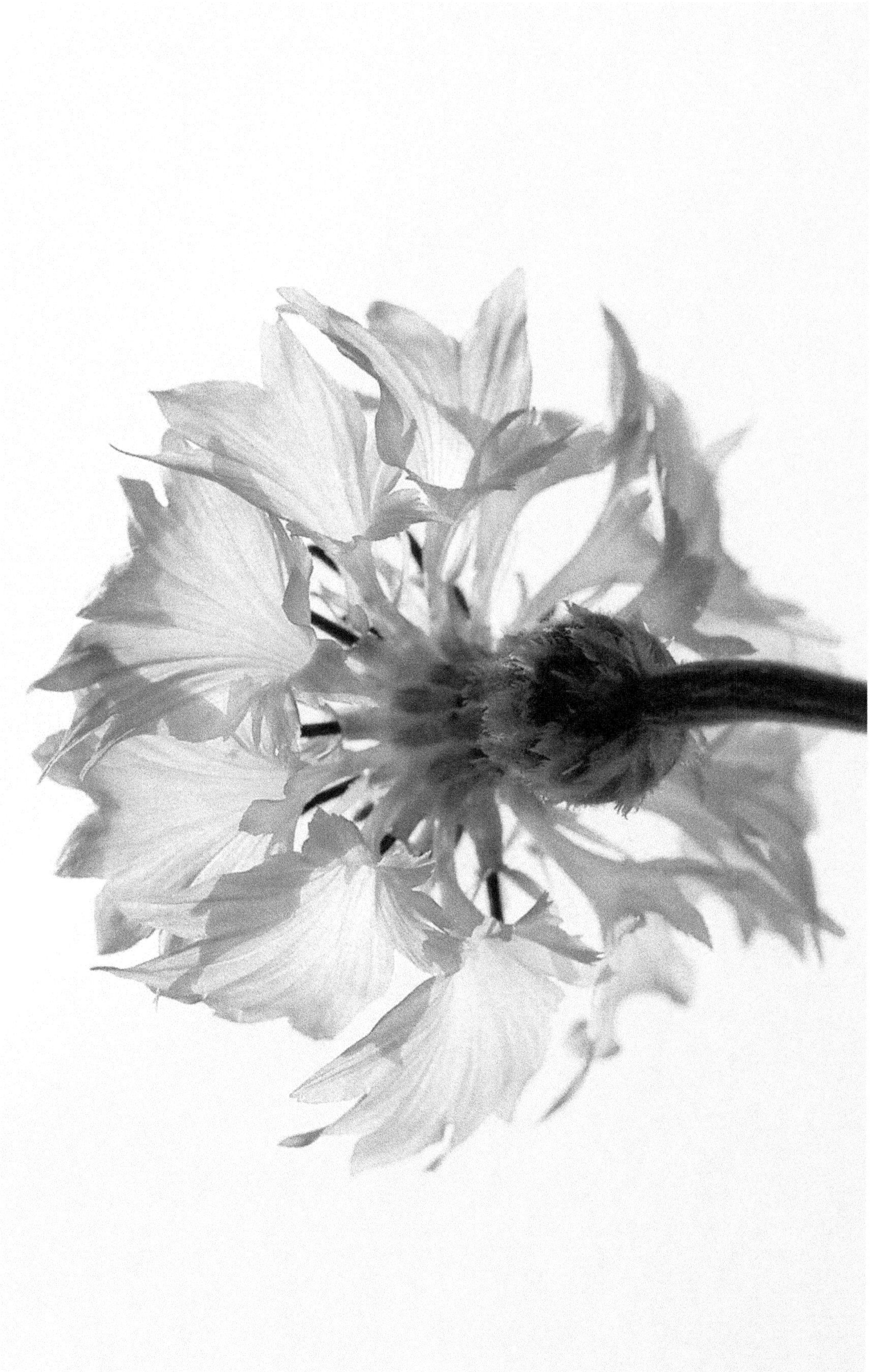

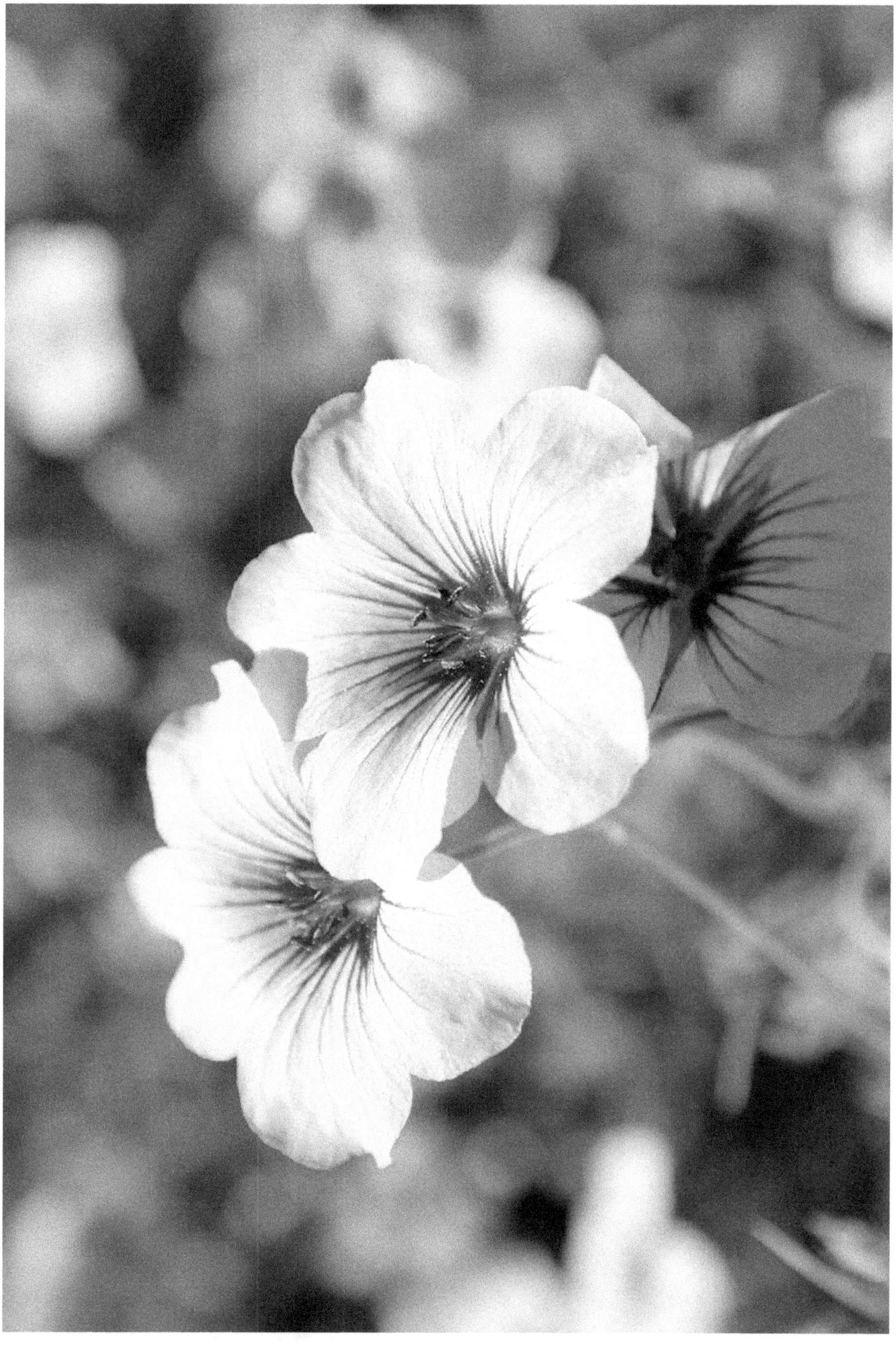

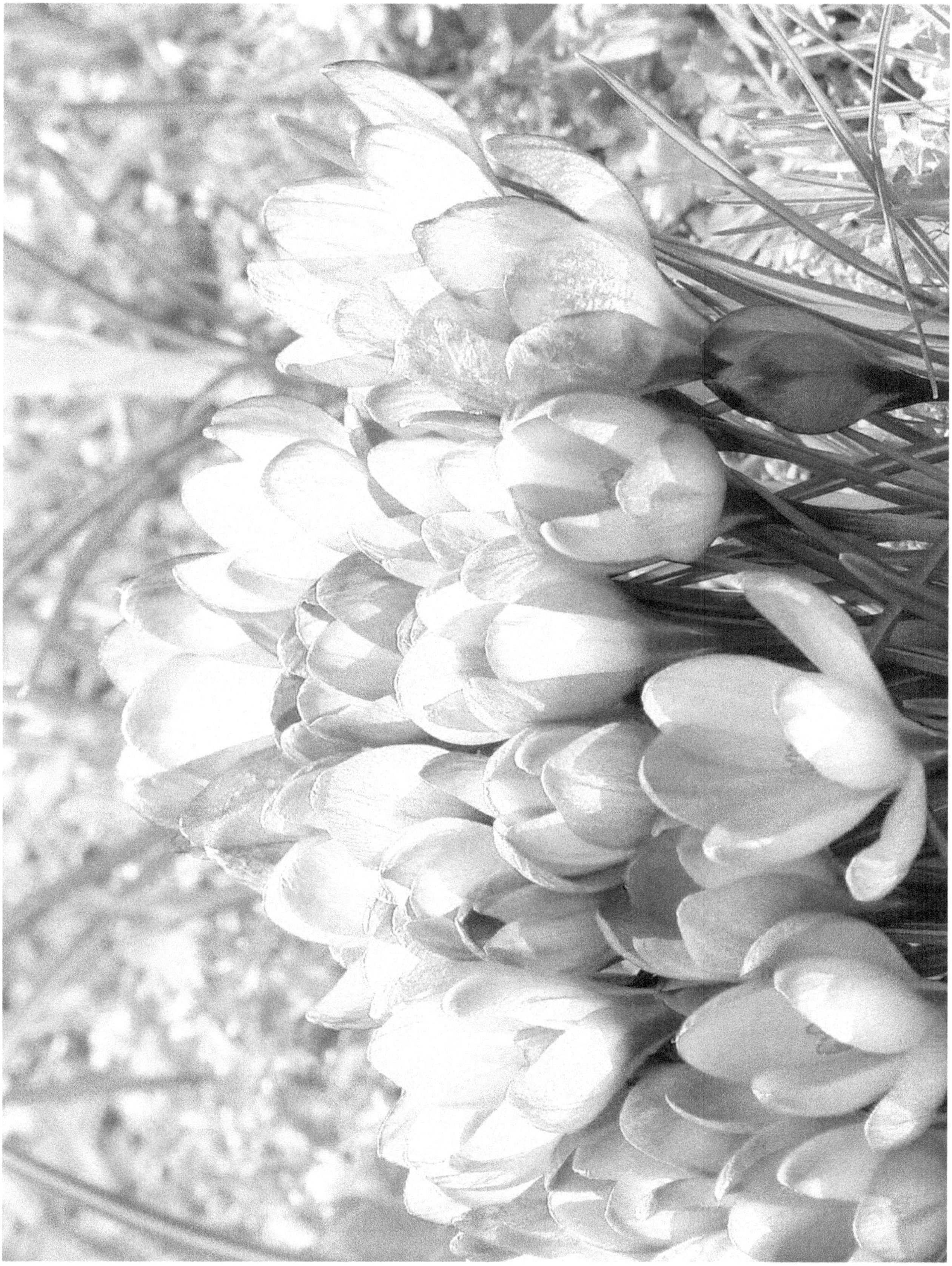

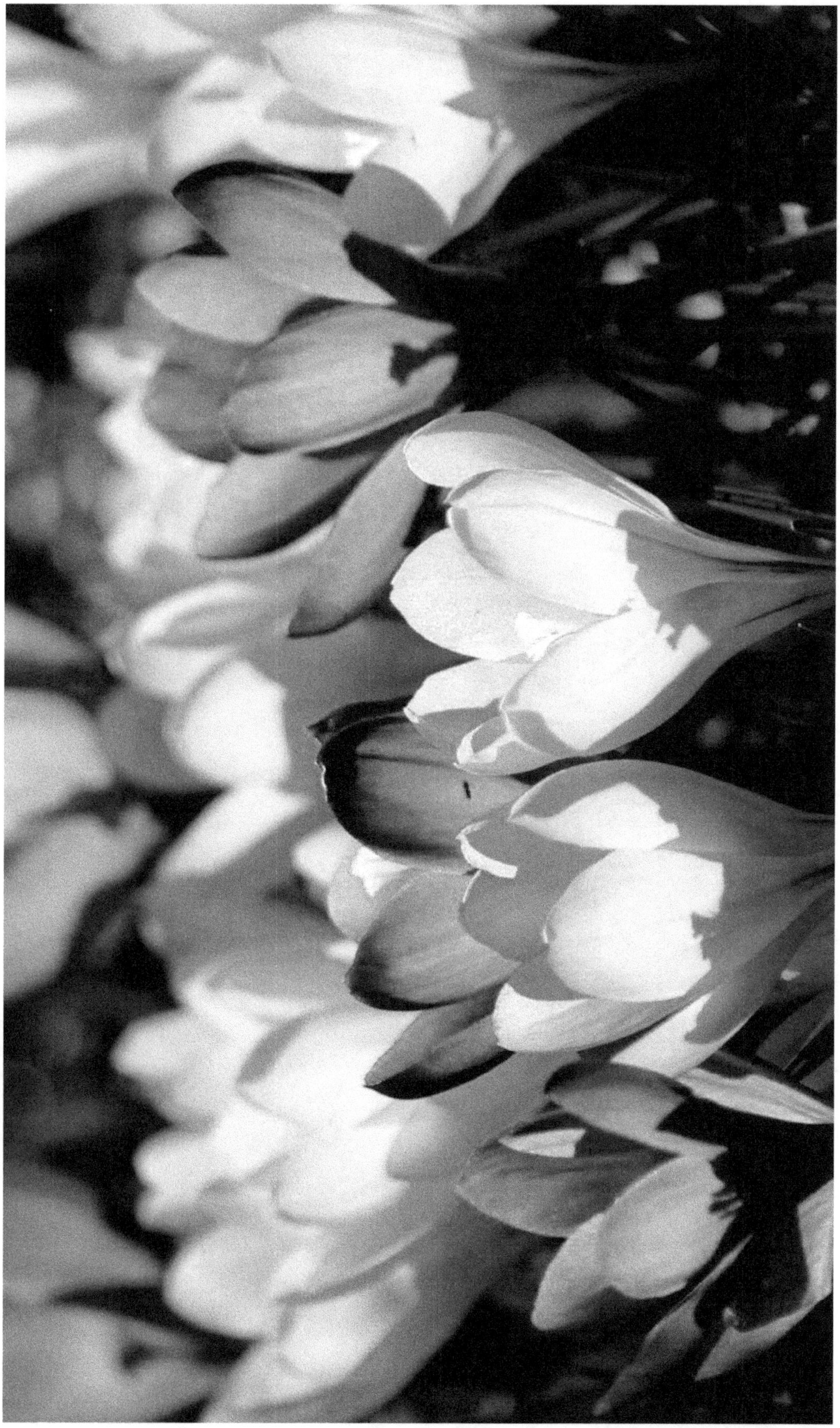

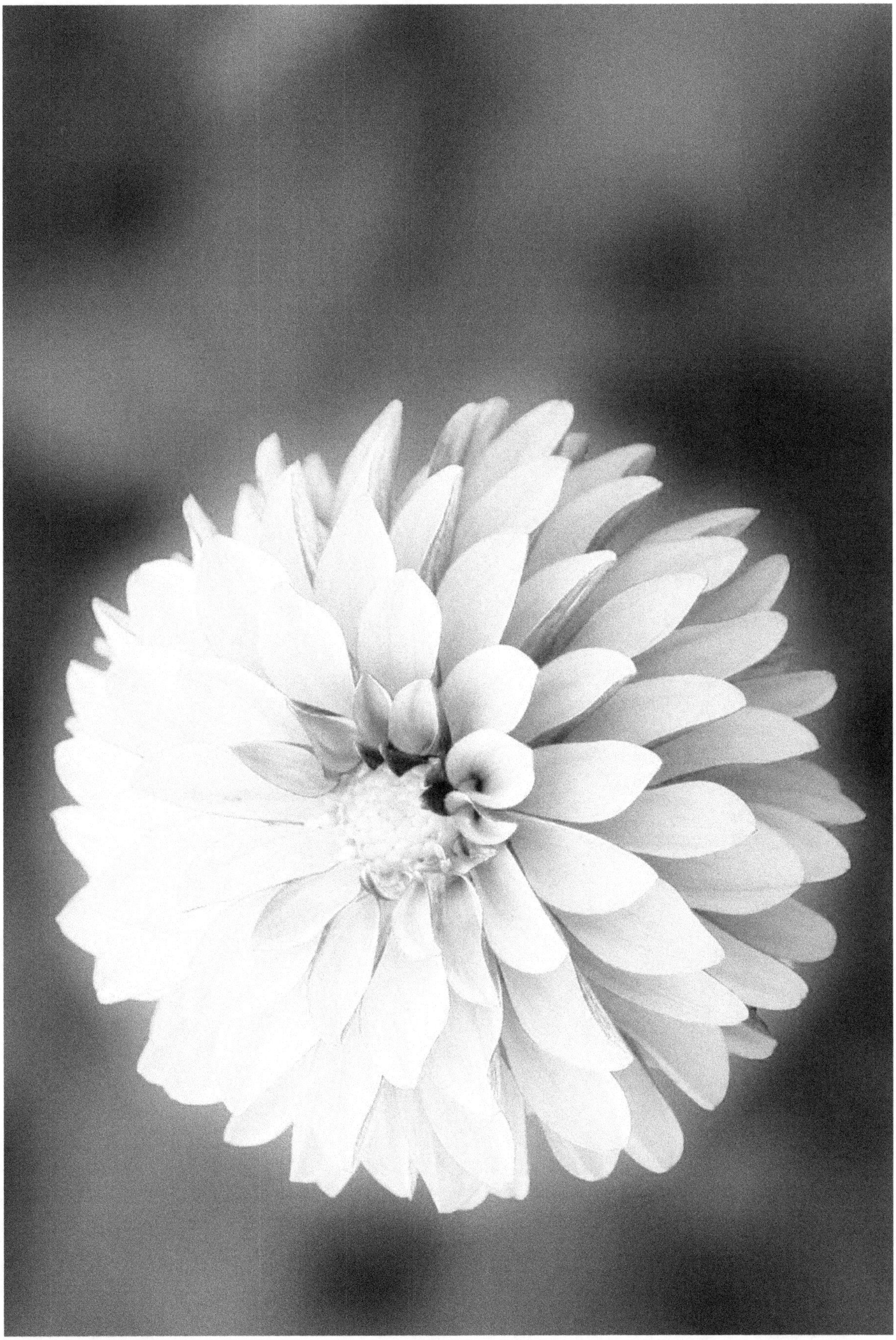

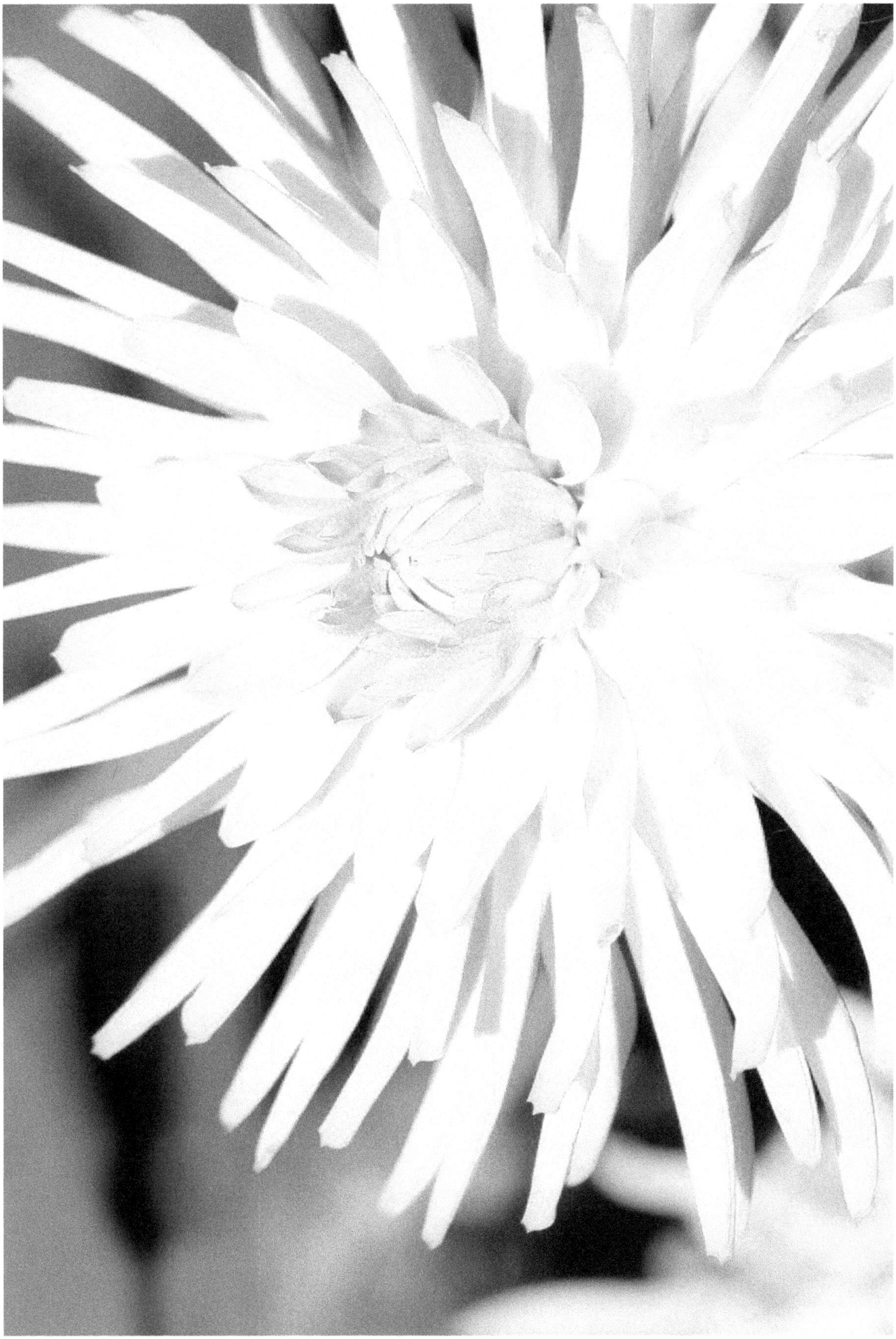

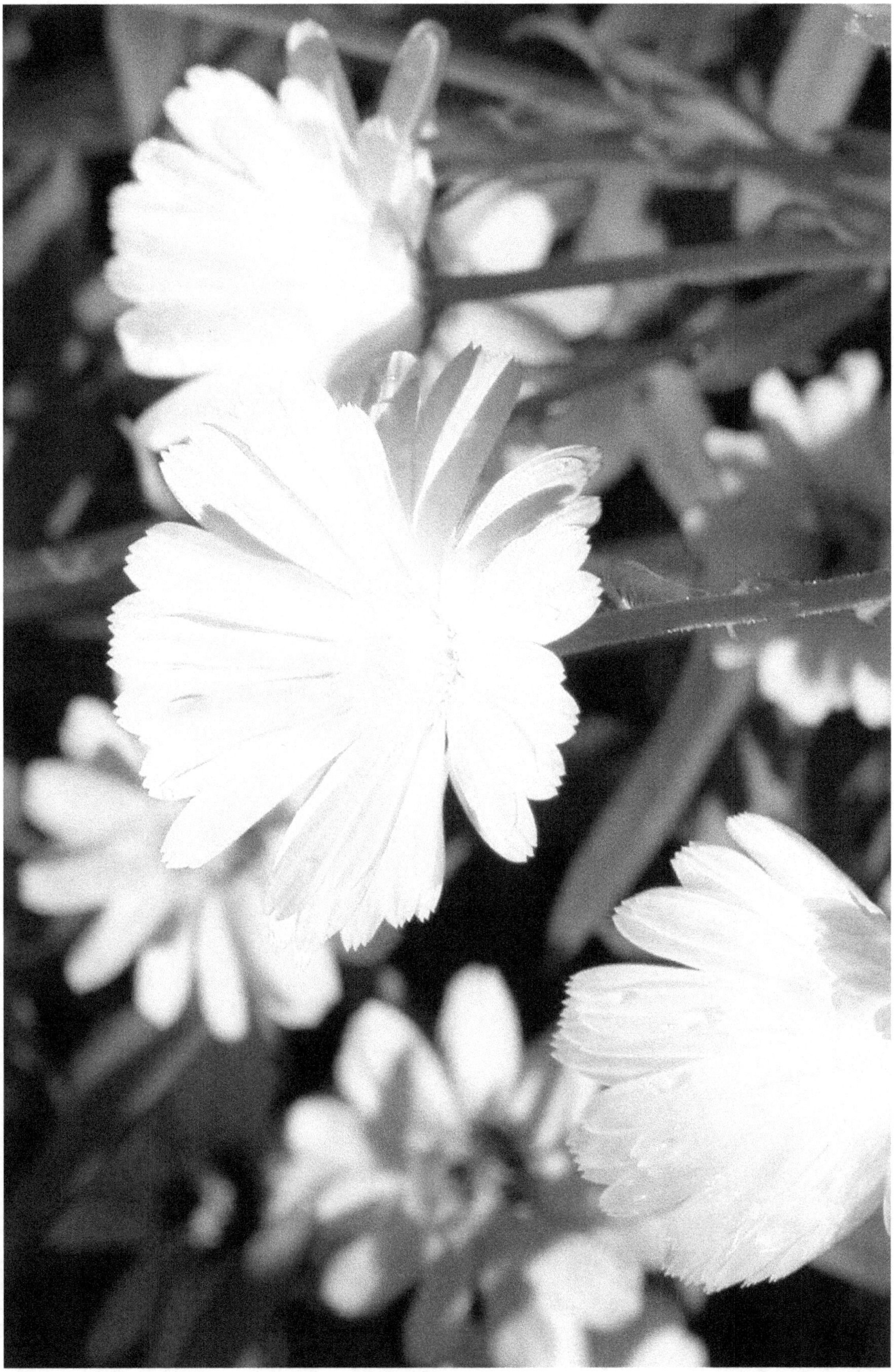

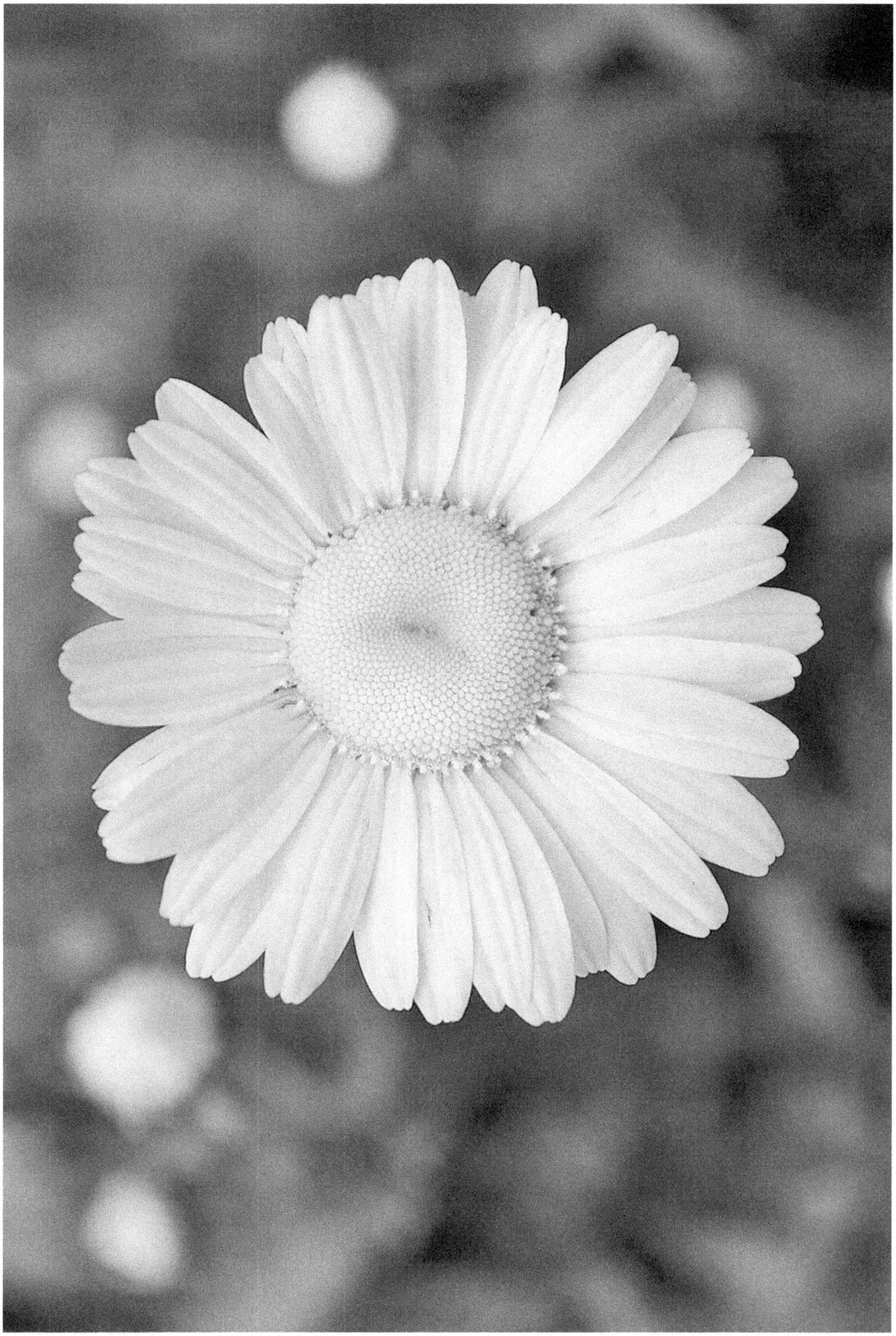

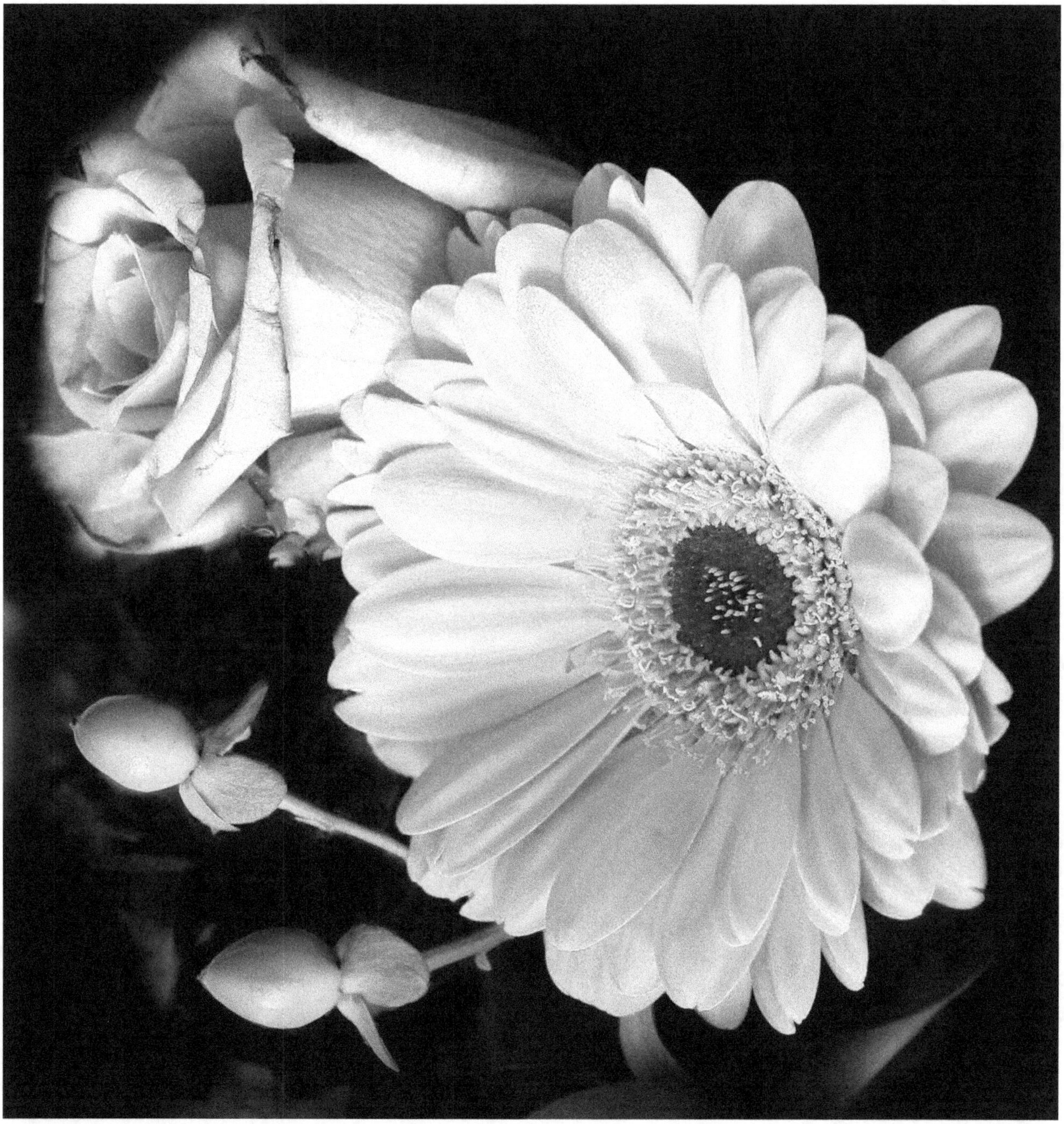

www.ingramcontent.com/pod-product-compliance
Lightning Source LLC
Chambersburg PA
CBHW080556190526
45169CB00007B/2798
9781535135962